Reading Skills

Grade 1

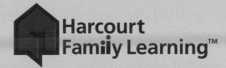
Harcourt
Family Learning™

FLASH KIDS and the distinctive Flash Kids logo are registered trademarks of Barnes & Noble Booksellers, Inc.
Harcourt Family Learning and Design is a trademark of Harcourt, Inc.

© 2004 by Flash Kids
Adapted from *Steck-Vaughn Core Skills: Reading Comprehension*
by Martha K. Resnick, Carolyn J. Hyatt, and Sylvia E. Freiman
© 2002 by Harcourt Achieve
Licensed under special arrangement with Harcourt Achieve.

For more information, please visit flashkids.com
Please submit all inquiries to Flashkids@sterlingpublishing.com

ISBN 978-1-4114-0113-6

Manufactured in China

Lot #:
40 42 44 46 45 43 41 39
08/17

Illustrator: Mark Stephens and Heidi Chang

New York

Dear Parent,

The ability to read well is an important part of your child's development. According to the National Institutes of Heath, students who are behind in reading in the third grade have only a 12 to 20 percent chance of ever catching up to the appropriate reading level. For this reason, it is crucial that your child master the basics of reading at an early age.

You have selected a unique book that focuses on developing your child's comprehension skills. Because this series was designed by experienced reading professionals, it encourages reading successes while building a firm understanding of the necessary skills outlined in national education standards.

Reading should be a fun, relaxed activity for children. They should read stories that relate to or build on their own experiences. The wide range of high-interest stories in this book will hold your child's attention and help develop his or her proficiency in reading. Other important features in this series that will further help your child include:

- Short reading selections of interest to a young reader.

- Vocabulary introduced in context and repeated often.

- Comprehension skills applied in context to make the reading more relevant.

- Multiple choice exercises that develop skills for standardized test taking.

You may wish to have your child read the selections silently or orally, but you will find that sharing the stories and activities with your child will provide additional confidence and support to succeed. When learners experience success, learning becomes a continuous process moving them toward higher achievements. Moreover, the more your child reads, the better he or she will become at reading. Continue your child's educational development at home with these fun activities:

- Enlist your child's help when writing grocery lists.

- When preparing a meal, have your child read the recipe aloud.

- Instead of reading a bedtime story to your child, have your child read a bedtime story to you!

- Write down the directions to a project, such as a gardening project or an arts and crafts project, for your child to read.

- Give your child a fun reading passage and ask him or her to draw a picture about it.

- Ask your child to read road signs and billboards that you encounter during car trips.

- Leave cute notes for your child on the refrigerator, under your child's pillow, or in his or her lunchbox.

- Have your child write and mail a letter to a loved one.

- Ask your child to read the directions for a board game, and then play the game together.

- Bring your child to the library or bookstore so that she or he can choose which great book to read next.

Table of Contents

unit 1

unit 2

unit 3

unit 4

unit 5

unit 6

unit 1

LESSON 1

Here Is a Spider

Here is a spider.
The spider can work.
The spider can make a new house.

See the new home.
The spider says,
"Walk in here, bugs.
Walk in the new house."

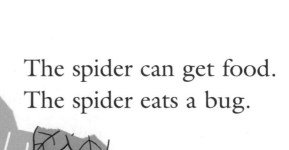

The spider can get food.
The spider eats a bug.

Read each question. Write **yes** or **no**.

1. Can a house walk?

no

2. Can a spider eat bugs?

yes

3. Can people walk?

yes

4. Can children eat?

yes

5. Can a house work
   for food?

no

6. Can a spider make
   a new home?

yes

7. Can a spider walk?

yes

Read the words. Match the picture to the right word. One is done for you.

house

food

people

Mom and Dad Work

See Jill and Mom.
Mom works.
Here is what Mom can do.

See Will and Mom.
Mom can work.
See what Mom can do.

Here are Nan and Dad.
See Dad work.
Dad works and works.

See Dan and Dad.
Dad is working.
Dad works here.

Who? What? Draw a line under the right one.

1. Who can make a house?

2. What cannot walk?

3. Who can eat?

   home   dad   live

4. What lives here?

   says   see   spider

5. Who can walk?

   food   mom   new

6. Who are people?

   a house   children and dad   walk and walk

7. Who can get a new house?

   mom and dad   live and eat   food and work

8. What cannot eat?

   house   children   people

Read the words. Put an **X** on the people.

Dan	Will	houses	not
walk	Mom	live	Dad
for	home	Nan	is
children	eat	food	get
do	new	Jill	in

Draw a circle around the right words.

1.

cannot walk

can eat

2.

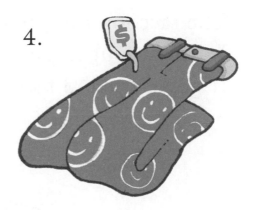

can make food

is in a house

3.

works in a house

can eat

4.

is not new

is new

The Tree Is a Home

See the tree.
The tree is a home.
What can live in the house?

See what lives here.
It is for a raccoon.
Raccoons can live in trees.

The raccoon can go in.
It can go out to get food.
It gets corn and fish to eat.

Draw a line under the best name for this story.

1. A House for a Fish
2. The Raccoon's Home
3. The Tree's Food

Read each story. Draw a line under
the best name for the story.

Will gets a fish to eat.
The raccoon sees Will.
It walks to Will.
Will says, "No, Raccoon!
The fish is for people."

1. The Raccoon Gets Food
    Will Eats the Raccoon
    Food for People

Dad Raccoon says,
"Walk in! Here is corn.
Eat and eat.
No people are here."

2. The People Eat Food
    The Raccoons Get Food
    The Raccoons Get Fish

Read each sentence. Write **yes** or **no**.

1. A tree can have fish in it.

2. Raccoons can get
    a new home.

3. Corn is food for raccoons.

4. Jill can eat corn and fish.

5. Trees can eat raccoons.

6. A fish can eat.

7. Corn can walk out to a tree.

Many Bees Live Here

What lives here?
Can children live here?
No. It is a home for bees.
Many bees live here.

Many bees work here.
They go to the flowers.
They take something from the flowers.

Bees take something into the house.
They make food from it.
The food is good to eat.
People will eat what the bees make.
What food do bees make?

Can they get home?
Draw a line to the right home.

1.

2.

3.

4.

5.

Write the best word to finish the sentence.

1. Bees go to the _____.   _____

     from   flowers

2. From flowers bees get _____.   _____

     something   see

3. Bees take something _____.   _____

     home   have

4. Bees make _____.   _____

     flowers   food

5. The food is _____.   _____

     go   good

6. People will eat _____.   _____

     it   is

7. Corn is something to _____.   _____

     it   eat

Reading Roundup

Draw a line under the right one.

1. Who can take a walk?

2. What can make something?

3. What cannot eat?

   raccoons   hills   bees

4. What can people do?
   make a new ant
   make a new house
   make a new raccoon

5. Which are **not** people?
   Nan and Dan
   bugs and flowers
   many children

Read each story. Draw a circle around a good name for it.

Raccoons eat corn and fish.
Ants eat many foods.
Fish eat bugs.

1. Who Can Walk?

2. What Animals Eat

3. What Bugs Eat

The children take a walk.
They go to the flowers.
They get many flowers.
They take the flowers to Mom.

1. The Flowers Walk

2. Mom Takes a Walk

3. Something for Mom

What do you see? Draw a circle around the right ones.
There are two right ones for each picture.

1. Raccoons live in the flowers.

2. Bees take something
   from flowers.

3. Bees work here.

4. The bees make a home.

1. Dan gets something new.

2. Dan gets something to eat.

3. Dan sees something new here.

4. Dan takes a walk.

The tree is a home.
It is a house.
See what lives here.

Here is the squirrel's home.
One squirrel lives here.
The squirrel climbs the tree.

Two birds live here.
They fly home.

What lives here?
Bugs live here.
Little bugs climb the tree.

What is at home here? Write the words in
the correct spaces. Use the words in the box.

squirrel   raccoon   children   bird   people

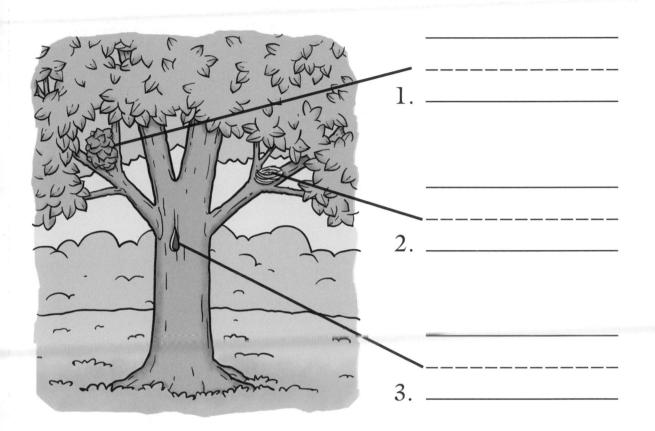

1. _____

2. _____

3. _____

4. _____

5. _____

Read each question. Circle **yes** or **no**.

1. Can a squirrel climb?   yes no

2. Can trees fly?   yes no

3. Can two flowers make a house?   yes no

4. Can two little children climb trees?   yes no

5. Can one raccoon live in a tree?   yes no

6. Can one squirrel take a walk?   yes no

7. Can fish live in hills?   yes no

8. Do bugs climb?   yes no

9. Do hills fly?   yes no

10. Is corn something good to eat?   yes no

LESSON 2 See the Duck!

Here is a pond.
What can be in a pond?
Many animals can live here.

Ducks live here.
The ducks look for food.
They look in the water.

See the duck!
Look at its food.
Fish live in water.
Little fish can be food for ducks.

What can be in the pond?

bugs

flowers

frogs

Read the story on page 23. Then answer the questions below by putting a ✔ by the right answer. One is done for you.

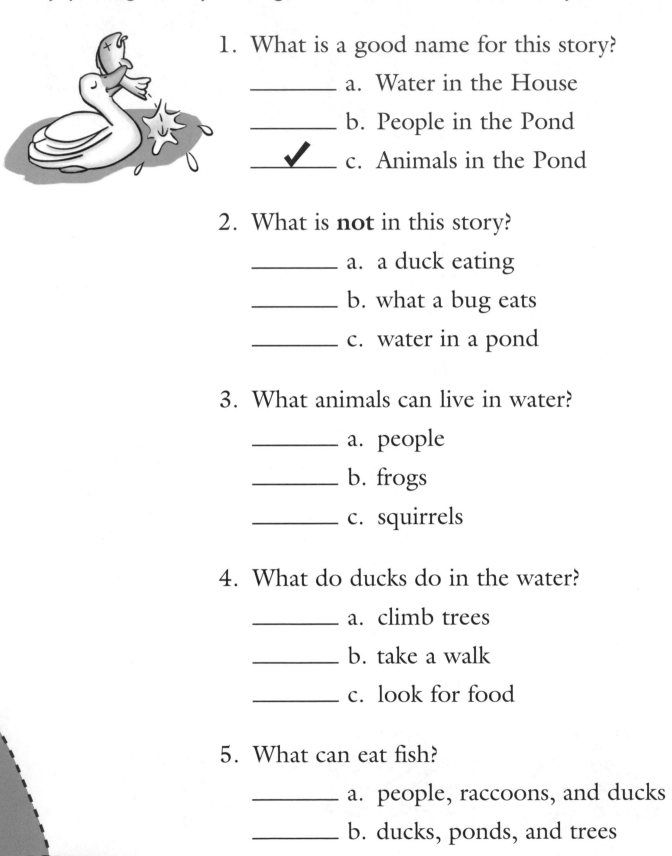

1. What is a good name for this story?

_____ a. Water in the House

_____ b. People in the Pond

___✔___ c. Animals in the Pond

2. What is **not** in this story?

_____ a. a duck eating

_____ b. what a bug eats

_____ c. water in a pond

3. What animals can live in water?

_____ a. people

_____ b. frogs

_____ c. squirrels

4. What do ducks do in the water?

_____ a. climb trees

_____ b. take a walk

_____ c. look for food

5. What can eat fish?

_____ a. people, raccoons, and ducks

_____ b. ducks, ponds, and trees

_____ c. flowers, trees, and houses

Look at the pictures. Read the sentences.
Match each picture to the best sentence.

a.

b.

1. The frog is not in the pond.

2. Two people play in the water.

3. It looks for something to eat.

c.

4. The fish eats the flower.

5. The bug can fly.

d.

Many Animals Live in Ponds

Many animals live in ponds.
They have to swim.
See the grass by the pond.
Animals can live in the grass.

Frogs live in the pond.
They go into the grass too.

Ducks can be in the grass.
They can go into the water too.

Many animals play in the water.
Many animals play by the water.
They have fun.

Read each sentence. Draw a line under the correct picture. One is done for you.

1. Mom can swim.

a.    b.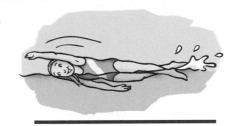

2. I have fun.

a.    b.

3. Children play by a tree.

a.    b.

4. Bees fly home.

a.    b.

5. Fish can live here.

a.    b.

Draw a circle around the right one.

1. Who lives in a hill?

    are   ant   out

2. Who will eat corn?

    be   by   bird

3. What is something to eat?

    can   corn   climb

4. Who can live in water?

    dad   duck   do

5. Who gets something from flowers?

    bee   be   by

6. Who can have fun?

    play   pond   people

7. Who can have a home?

    are   ant   out

The bug says, "Look! I am big."
The bird says, "No! **I** am big.
You are little."

The bird says, "I am little."
The fox says, "Yes, you are little.
I am big."

Dad says, "Look here, Fox.
I am big.
You are the little one."
The fox says, "I can look.
I can see you.
You are the big one."

Draw a line from each sentence to the correct picture.
One is done for you.

a.   ——————— 1. I am big.

b.   2. I am little.

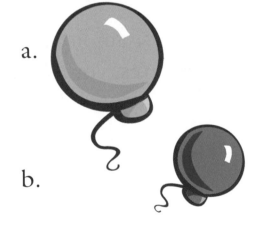

a.   3. It is something little.

b.   4. It is something big.

---

a.    5. See the little one.

b. 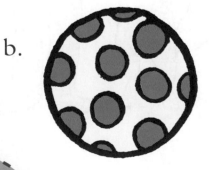   6. See the big one.

Write the best word to finish the sentence.

1. The bird looks for food.

   _____

   ---------------   children   bugs
   It will eat _____ .

2. Here is something good to eat.

   _____

   ---------------   fish   fly
   People will eat _____ .

3. A fox will climb.

   _____

   ---------------   hill   pond
   It can climb a _____ .

4. Animals can have fun.

   _____

   ---------------   play   pond
   They will _____ .

5. The frogs have fun in the water.

   _____

   ---------------   swim   fly
   They will _____ .

Write the name of each thing in the picture. Use these words.

grass   fish   duck   raccoon   flower   frog

1. _____

2. _____

3. _____

4. _____

5. _____

6. _____

Read each story. Draw a circle around a good name for it.

The fox and the frog play.
They play by the water.
They play in the grass.
They have fun.

1. The Fox Eats

2. The Animals Have Food

3. The Animals Have Fun

The fox says, "I will get something good to eat."
The frog says, "You will not get a frog to eat."
The frog gets into the water.
A little frog can swim.
A fox cannot swim.

1. The Fox Will Not Eat a Frog

2. The Fox Eats a Frog

3. The Fox Gets a Duck

Write the best word to finish the sentence.

1. Mom will go out to play. Mom will have _____.

          fly   fun

2. Jill has something to eat. Jill has _____.

      corn   climb

3. The flower is little. A flower cannot _____.

    something   swim

4. Dad has something new. Dad says, "It is for _____."

      you   out

5. The spider has a web. The spider will get _____.

    hills   bugs

unit 3

The Home Is in the Ground

Chipmunk says, "I have a good house.
It is in the ground by the rocks."
A big fox says, "I want to see
where Chipmunk lives."

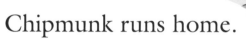

Chipmunk runs home.
The home is in the ground.

The fox says,
"I see where
Chipmunk lives.
I want to eat. I will
get into Chipmunk's house."
The fox is not happy.
She says, "I am too big.
I cannot get into the little home."

Make a circle around the best ending for each sentence.

1. The fox wants to get into the chipmunk's house.
   She wants to

   a. play with the chipmunk.

   b. swim with the chipmunk.

   c. get food.

2. The fox cannot get into the chipmunk's home.
   The fox says,

   a. "I will not eat a duck."

   b. "I will not eat a chipmunk."

   c. "I will eat good rocks."

Write the word to finish the sentence.
Use the words in the box.

| fox | lives | run | ground |

_____

1. A chipmunk's house is in the _____.

_____

2. The chipmunk can _____.

_____

3. Here is where the animal _____.

Underline the words that match the picture.

1.

not on the ground

on the ground

2.

happy people

happy ducks

3.

the rock

two rocks

4.

a frog by a bug

a frog by a flower

5.

on the grass

on the water

6.

is a bird

is not a bird

Here Comes a Snake

Chipmunk says, "I am happy.
The fox cannot get me."

Here comes a snake.
She says, "I am not too big.
I will get into Chipmunk's house.
I like to eat little animals."
Chipmunk sees the snake.
She runs back into her house fast.

The snake is fast too.
She is in Chipmunk's house.

Chipmunk says, "The snake cannot get me.
I have a back door to my house!
The back door is by the rocks."

Read the story on page 37.
<u>Underline</u> the best name for the story.

1. Food for a Chipmunk

2. A Snake in the House

3. Food for a Fox

Write the word to finish the sentence.
Use the words in the box.

| fast   me   rocks   door |

1. A chipmunk runs _____.

2. She runs out the _____.

3. The back door is by the _____.

What came first in the story? Write **1** in the box next to it.
What came next? Write **2**. What came last? Write **3**.

☐ Chipmunk runs out the back door.

☐ Chipmunk runs into the house.

☐ Snake gets into Chipmunk's house.

38

What will come next? Put a ✔ by it.
One is done for you.

1. The snakes have no food.

    _____ a. They are happy.

    ✔ b. They look for something to eat.

    _____ c. They go to live with a spider.

2. The frogs are in the pond.

    _____ a. They will run.

    _____ b. They will walk.

    _____ c. They will swim.

3. The bugs have a home in the tree.

    _____ a. They have to climb.

    _____ b. They have to swim.

    _____ c. They can get a fish.

4. The spider works to make a new house.

    _____ a. She will get bugs to eat.

    _____ b. She will get a bird.

    _____ c. She will live in the ant hill.

5. The snake gets into Chipmunk's house.

    _____ a. The snake works with Chipmunk.

    _____ b. The chipmunk and snake play.

    _____ c. The chipmunk runs out the back door.

It Is Cold

The duck says, "It is cold.
You will not see me, dog.
I will go away. Good-bye."

The dog says, "Where will you go?"
The duck says, "Where it is not cold."

The frog says, "Good-bye, dog.
I will go away too. It is too cold."
The dog says, "Where will you go, frog?"

Frog says, "I go under the water here.
I get into the mud.
I will sleep in the mud."

The dog sees the duck fly away.
He sees the frog swim away.

The dog says, "It is cold.
I will go into my house."

Draw a circle around the answer to each question.

1. What is this story about?

   a. Dogs sleep under the water.

   b. A cat is under the flowers.

   c. Animals want to go away.

2. What is not in the story?

   a. The dog says, "It is cold."

   b. A cat sleeps in the mud.

   c. A duck can fly away.

Where is the bird? Draw a line from
the words to the correct picture.

1.    under a flower   2.

on the corn

3.    on a squirrel   4.

on the hill

5.    on a raccoon   6.

in a spider's home

Make a circle around the answer to each question.

1. What cannot fly away?

2. What do raccoons eat?

3. Where is something under a tree?

4. What can you climb?

Reading Roundup

Underline the sentence that answers the question.
One is done for you.

1. What makes Dan happy?

    a. He has new flowers.

    b. He has a new animal.

2. Where is the bird?

    a. It plays by the tree.

    b. It is in its home.

3. Where is the bee?

    a. It is under the flower.

    b. It is on the flower.

4. Who can sleep?

    a. A door can sleep.

    b. A dog can sleep.

Read the story. Underline the best name for the story.

The children want
something to eat.
They get food they like.
They play and run fast.
They have fun.

1. The Happy People

2. The Happy Rocks

3. By the Door

Write the best word to answer the question.

1. Where do frogs sleep?

_____

－－－－－－－－－－

_____

mom   mud   many

2. What can go fast?

_____

－－－－－－－－－

_____

a rock a snake ground

3. Where can ducks fly?

_____

－－－－－－－－－

_____

away   and   are

4. What cannot be happy?

_____

－－－－－－－－

_____

a door birds children

5. What do spiders
want to eat?

_____

－－－－－－－－

_____

people rocks bugs

6. Where do ants
want to live?

_____

－－－－－－－－

_____

a door a hill a pond

Underline the best answer.

1.   The bird wants to eat ants.

   a. So the ants have to run fast.

   b. So the ants play with the bird.

   c. So the ants eat the bird.

2. We like to fish.

   a. So we fly into the tree.

   b. So we live by the water.

   c. So we look for fish in the ground.

44

Write the word to finish the sentence. Use the words in the box.

ground	want	happy	fast

1. People have fun. They are _____ .

2. She can run _____ .

3. What do you _____ ?

Read the story. What came first? Write **1** in the box next to it.
What came next? Write **2**. What came last? Write **3**.

Dan says, "I do not want a big rock here.
I will take it out." He gets the rock out.
Dan sees a big snake on the ground.
He turns and runs home.

☐ He runs home fast.

☐ He sees a big snake.

☐ Dan wants the rock out.

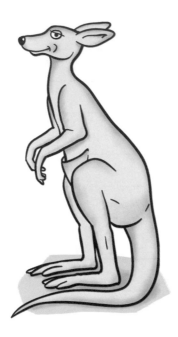

This animal has a big tail.
It has big back paws.
It jumps on its back feet.
Its front paws are like hands.

Look at your little finger.
This animal's new baby is that little.
The baby has no fur. It cannot see.
It lives in the mother's pouch.
It lives there a long time.
It gets big in the pouch.
What animal is this?

It is a kangaroo.

Which one is right? Put a ✔ by it. One is done for you.

1. What has a pouch?

    _____ a. a new baby

    _____ b. your hand

    ___✔___ c. the mother animal

2. What animal is this?

    _____ a. kangaroo

    _____ b. rabbit

    _____ c. lion

3. Where must a new baby kangaroo live?

    _____ a. in an egg

    _____ b. in the mother's pouch

    _____ c. in a nest

4. How do these animals walk?

    _____ a. on four paws

    _____ b. on three paws

    _____ c. on two paws

5. What is a good name for this story?

    _____ a. A Little Finger

    _____ b. A Funny Animal

    _____ c. A Little Bunny

6. What do you know about the new baby?

    _____ a. It has brown fur.

    _____ b. It has no back paws.

    _____ c. It cannot see.

Draw lines to match the words.
One is done for you.

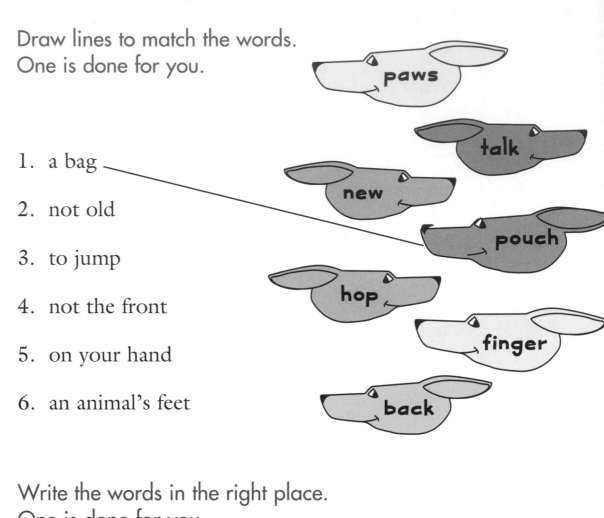

1. a bag

2. not old

3. to jump

4. not the front

5. on your hand

6. an animal's feet

Write the words in the right place.
One is done for you.

paw   pouch   fur

tail   hop   back   front

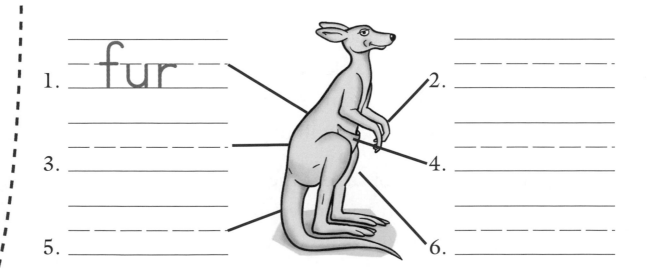

1. fur

2. _____

3. _____

4. _____

5. _____

6. _____

Who? What?

Circle the right words. One is done for you.

1.   Kangaroos are funny animals.

She
(They)   jump far.

2.   The new baby cannot see.

It
They   cannot jump.

3.   The mother kangaroo has a pouch.

He
She   has a baby in the pouch.

4.   The kangaroo's tail is big.

She
It   is not little.

5.   Father kangaroo lives far away.

He
She   can hop fast.

6.   Baby kangaroos have no fur.

It
They   will get fur soon.

7.   The pouch is on the kangaroo.

It
They   has a baby in it.

The Ducks Have Food

One day Mother Duck walked.
She walked on the grass.

She said, "Let's swim in the water.
You will do something new.
Do what I do.
It will be fun."

The ducks have food.
They got it in the pond.
The little ducks did something new.

Which one is right? Put a ✔ by it. One is done for you.

1.   When did this story happen?

   __✔__   a. day

   _____   b. night

   _____   c. at the pond

2. Where did Mother Duck take the baby ducks?

   _____   a. to the farm

   _____   b. to the water

   _____   c. to school

3. What new thing did the baby ducks do?

   _____   a. get food

   _____   b. go to sleep

   _____   c. play a game

4. How do baby ducks learn?

   _____   a. by reading a book

   _____   b. by eating fish

   _____   c. by looking at big ducks

5. What is the best name for this story?

   _____   a. Baby Ducks Can Fly

   _____   b. Baby Ducks Run Away

   _____   c. Baby Ducks Do Something New

Draw lines to match the words.
One is done for you.

1. not old

2. something to eat

3. to go fast in the water

4. some water

5. a good time

6. something feet can do

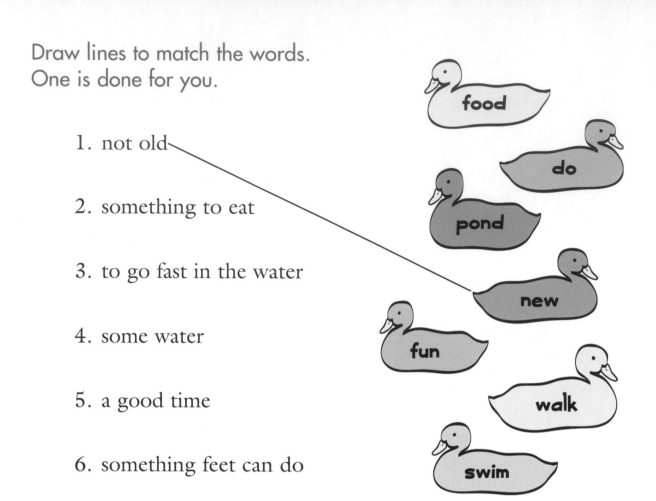

food

do

pond

new

fun

walk

swim

Each picture goes with a sentence.
Draw lines to match them.

1.

2.

3.

Flowers are in the pond.

A duck is flying.

Ducks swim.

The duck walks with Mother Duck.

A duck is eating.

Who? What? Circle the right word. One is done for you.

1. The ducks are on the grass.

She
(They)

   are walking.

2. The flower was in the pond.

It
He

   was white.

3. Fish can swim.

We
They

   can go fast.

4. Ann is by the water.

He
She

   looks at the fish.

5. Tim can swim.

He
They

   can have fun.

Can you tell the story? Some things are not in the right place. Put **1**, **2**, and **3** in the boxes. One is done for you.

☐   The ducks went into the water.

☐   They got food.

1   The ducks walked on the grass.

Lesson 3 — The Robins Were Working

One morning the robins were working.
They were making a nest.
The nest was in an old oak tree.
Mr. Robin found some grass for the nest.
Mrs. Robin got mud for the nest.
The nest was made of mud and grass.
Soon Mrs. Robin will lay eggs in the nest.
The eggs will be blue.
What will come out of the robins' eggs?

Which one is right? Put a ✔ by it.

1. When were the robins working?

_____ a. at night

_____ b. at noon

_____ c. in the morning

2. What were the robins making?

_____ a. a school

_____ b. a home

_____ c. an oak tree

3. Where was the nest?

    _____ a. in an apple tree

    _____ b. in the brown sand

    _____ c. in an oak tree

4. What was used to make the nest?

    _____ a. grass and mud

    _____ b. sand and mud

    _____ c. grass and sand

5. What will Mrs. Robin do?

    _____ a. dig a hole

    _____ b. lay eggs in the nest

    _____ c. play and run

6. What color is a robin's egg?

    _____ a. white   _____ b. brown   _____ c. blue

7. What will come out of robins' eggs?

    _____ a. baby chickens

    _____ b. baby birds

    _____ c. baby turtles

8. What is the best name for the story?

    _____ a. A Nest in the Sand

    _____ b. A Nest in a Tree

    _____ c. A Nest in the Grass

Draw lines to match these. One is done for you.

1. green plants

2. time of the day

3. kind of bird

4. what a woman is called

5. a tree

6. color of a robin's egg

7. what a man is called

8. home for birds

robin

morning

oak

Mrs.

grass

Mr.

nest

blue

make

Each picture goes with a sentence.
Draw lines to match them.

1.

2.

3.

The robin finds some grass.

Three eggs are in the nest.

The robins make a nest.

The oak tree is big.

Two eggs are in the nest.

Who? What?

Circle the right word for each story.

1. The eggs are blue.

   What will come out of | them / it | ?

2. Mr. Robin and Mrs. Robin made a nest.

   | They / She | got grass for the nest.

3. Mrs. Robin saw a man.

   Mrs. Robin went away from | them / him | .

4. The birds live in the tree.

   They have a nest in | it / them | .

5. Mrs. Robin will lay eggs soon.

   | Our / Her | eggs will be blue.

Can you tell the story? Some things are not in the right place. Put **1**, **2**, and **3** in the boxes. One is done for you.

☐ Mrs. Robin will lay eggs in the nest.

☐ They made a nest in the oak tree.

1 Mr. and Mrs. Robin got grass and mud.

57

Ann and Andy Went to the Store

One afternoon Mom wanted some food. Ann and Andy went to the store for her. They walked a long way down Duck Street. Then they went around a corner. They walked by the park. Then they got to the store.

Ann and Andy found eggs, bread, fish, and milk. A woman put the food into a bag for them. They gave the woman some money. Then Ann and Andy walked home.

When Mom looked inside the bag, she said, "You forgot the lettuce!"

Ann and Andy had to go all the way back to the store. Then they had to walk home again.

Which one is right? Put a ✔ by it.

1. Who went to the store?

_____ a. two children

_____ b. Mom

_____ c. two boys

2. When did they go to the store?

_____ a. at night

_____ b. in the morning

_____ c. in the afternoon

3. Where did the woman put the food?

_____ a. in a bag

_____ b. in a box

_____ c. in the park

4. What did Ann and Andy give the woman?

_____ a. food   _____ b. lettuce   _____ c. money

5. Why did Ann and Andy go back to the store?

_____ a. to get money

_____ b. to get lettuce

_____ c. to see Mom there

6. What do we know about the store?

_____ a. It was a long way from home.

_____ b. It was next to Ann and Andy's house.

_____ c. It was on Old Street.

7. What is the best name for this story?

_____ a. The Lost Lettuce

_____ b. Fun at the Store

_____ c. Two Long Walks

Draw lines to match these. One is done for you.

1. a place to play

2. did not think about

3. a green food

4. a white drink

5. used to pay for things

6. boys and girls

7. a time of day

8. where two streets come together

lettuce

milk

park

forgot

corner

duck

afternoon

children

money

Pick out the right word from the bag. Write the word. One is done for you.

walk   black   milk

day   house   girl

1. lettuce, bread, eggs,

   milk

2. school, store, home,

3. run, skip, jump,

4. Mom, woman, sister,

5. green, blue, brown,

Who? What?

Circle the right word for each story.

1. The lettuce was green.

   | It |
   | They |

   was in a brown bag.

2. Ann got some eggs.

   She wanted to eat

   | it |
   | them |

   .

3. The children went down Duck Street.

   | She |
   | They |

   went around the corner.

4. Andy had some money.

   | He |
   | She |

   gave it to a woman.

5. Ann walked with Andy.

   Ann was next to

   | her |
   | him |

   .

Can you tell the story? Some things are not in the right place. Put **1**, **2**, and **3** in the boxes.

☐ Ann and Andy forgot to get the lettuce.

☐ Mother wanted some food from the store.

3 Ann and Andy had to go back to the store.

Reading Roundup

Read the question. Write the answer next to each one.
How many paws do they have? Write the words.

zero   one   four

1. _____

2. _____

3. _____

4. _____

5. _____

6. _____

7. _____

8. _____

Who?
What? Circle the right word for each story.

1. Dad got some eggs at the store.

   [He / She] took the eggs home.

2. Ann and Andy ran around the corner.

   [They / She] ran fast.

3. Mom forgot to take the bags.

   She had to go home to get [it / them].

Draw lines to match these.

1. a kind of bag

2. something to eat

3. time after morning

4. one more time

5. place to play

6. time for bed

7. not the back

pouch

front

night

afternoon

food

milk

park

again

Read each sentence. Finish it. Circle the right picture.

1. Mrs. Robin will lay a blue _____ in the nest.

   a.    b.    c.

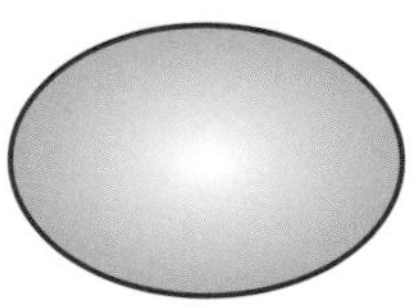

2. The kangaroo has a big _____.

   a.    b. 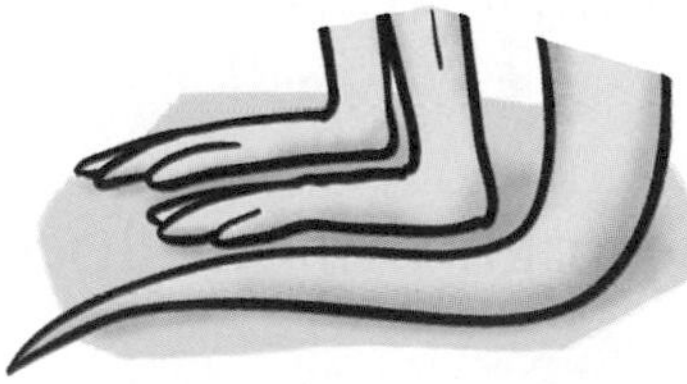   c.

3. The little ducks eat _____.

   a.    b.    c.

Circle the right word.

1. We saw the kangaroo
   $\boxed{\begin{array}{c} \text{hot} \\ \text{hop} \end{array}}$
   in the tall grass.

2. Robins make a nest of
   $\boxed{\begin{array}{c} \text{grass} \\ \text{green} \end{array}}$
   and
   $\boxed{\begin{array}{c} \text{mad} \\ \text{mud} \end{array}}$.

3. The dog had a bath in a
   $\boxed{\begin{array}{c} \text{but} \\ \text{tub} \end{array}}$.

4. Ann and Andy
   $\boxed{\begin{array}{c} \text{forgot} \\ \text{four} \end{array}}$
   the lettuce.

5. They had to go
   $\boxed{\begin{array}{c} \text{black} \\ \text{back} \end{array}}$
   to the store.

6. Mother gave them
   $\boxed{\begin{array}{c} \text{money} \\ \text{many} \end{array}}$
   to get food.

7. Mother Duck walked on the
   $\boxed{\begin{array}{c} \text{goats} \\ \text{grass} \end{array}}$.

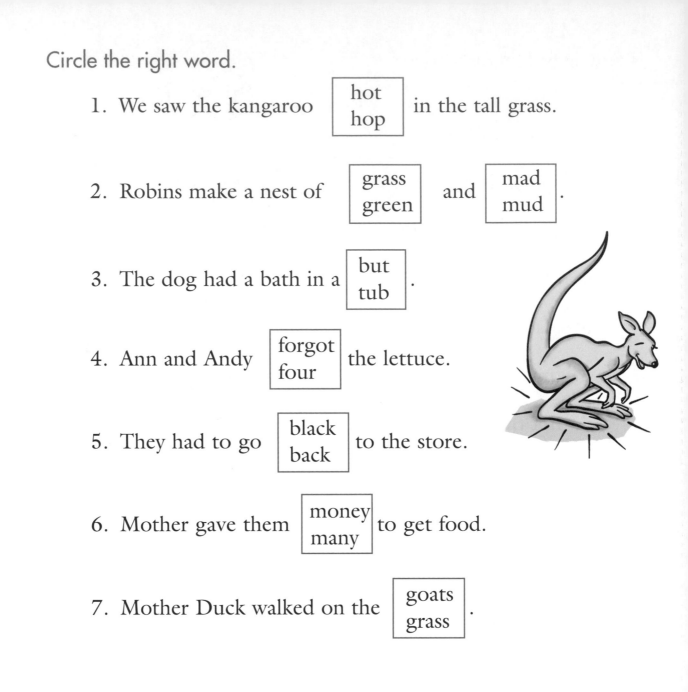

Can you tell about the story on page 58? Some things
are not in the right place. Put **1**, **2**, and **3** in the boxes.

☐ A woman put the food into a bag.

☐ Mom said, "You forgot the lettuce!"

☐ Ann and Andy walked to the store.

Each picture goes with a sentence. Draw lines to match them.

1.

    a. The baby gets big
       in the pouch.

2.

    b. People can get
       a bath in this tub.

3.

    c. The robins look
       for food.

4.

    d. The children got
       them at the store.

5.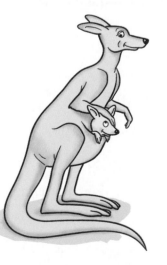

    e. The robins made a
       nest of grass and mud.

The Toy Shelf

Mom and Dad wanted the children to take care of their toys. Every night the children put all the big toys in their rooms. Then they put all the little toys on a toy shelf. Each child had a shelf.

Bob was ten. He had the top shelf. Bev was eight. She had the middle shelf. Bill was seven. He had the bottom shelf.

On Sunday evening, Dad and Mom found lots of toys on the rug. They went to look at the toy shelf. They saw no toys on the middle shelf.

Mom said, "Now I know who did not put the toys away."

Dad said, "I can guess who it is too."

Can you guess who forgot to put away toys?

Which one is right? Put a ✓ by it.

1.   What was the story about?

_____ a. getting a new rug

_____ b. getting a toy shelf

_____ c. a child who forgot to do something

2. What did Mom and Dad want the children to do?

_____ a. go to the store

_____ b. put away the toys

_____ c. make a new shelf

3. Where did the children put their big toys?

_____ a. on a shelf

_____ b. under a bed

_____ c. in their rooms

4. Where did Dad and Mom find some toys?

_____ a. on the chair

_____ b. on the rug

_____ c. at the store

5. When did Dad and Mom find toys on the rug?

_____ a. Tuesday evening

_____ b. Sunday evening

_____ c. Sunday afternoon

6. Who forgot to put the toys away?

_____ a. Bev

_____ b. Bill

_____ c. Bob

7. How did Mom know who did not put away toys?

_____ a. She saw toys on every shelf.

_____ b. She saw no toys on one shelf.

_____ c. She asked the children.

Draw lines to match these.

1. six and one

2. part that is under

3. day of the week

4. late in the day

5. seven and one

6. place to put things on

7. all of them

8. things to play with

9. not the top or
   the bottom

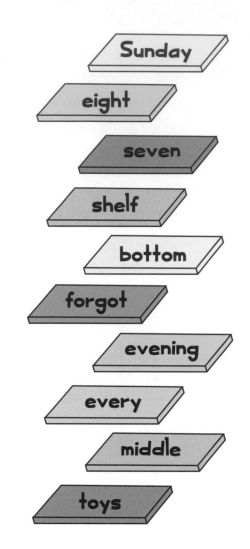

Put some things on the big shelf.

1. Put a blue ✖ on
   the middle shelf.

2. Put a brown ✔ on
   the bottom shelf.

3. Put a blue egg on
   the middle shelf.

4. Put a black box on
   the top shelf.

5. Put a red ▲ on
   every shelf.

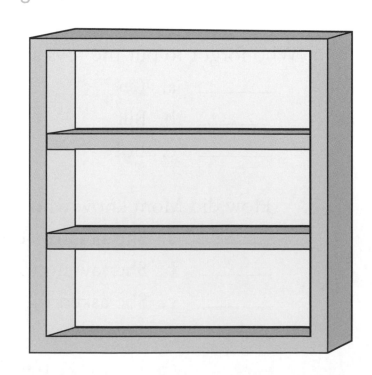

Circle one word that fits both sentences.

1. A bird sat on _____ of the tree.

   too   top

2. Bill played with his toy _____.

3. Mom and Dad went to see a _____.

   play   day

4. Children like to run and _____.

5. The children must take _____ of the toys.

   can   care

6. Bob did not _____ when Bev took his toy.

Look back at the story on page 66.
Put the right child's name on each line.

1. _____ was seven years old.

2. _____ was eight.

3. _____ was ten years old.

4. _____ had the top toy shelf.

5. _____ had the middle shelf.

6. _____ forgot to put away the toys.

Ducks in the Water

Ducks like to be in water. They can swim fast. They play games in the water. They find food there too. Ducks eat little bugs and fish. They pull plants out of the water to eat.

Ducks have big orange feet. The feet are good for pushing the water. Their feet make ducks good swimmers. Ducks' feet are not so good for walking and running. Their feet are not good for climbing.

Sometimes ducks must come out of the water. They cannot walk as well as they can swim. Ducks must take care on land. If ducks are not careful on land, a fox may catch them.

Why do you think a fox likes to catch a duck?

Which one is right? Put a ✓ by it.

1.   Why do foxes like to catch ducks?

_____   a. to make friends

_____   b. to play games

_____   c. for food

2. What do ducks like to eat?

_____ a. birds

_____ b. foxcs

_____ c. bugs and plants

3. What can ducks use their feet to do?

_____ a. climb trees

_____ b. push water

_____ c. talk fast

4. Why don't foxes catch ducks in the water?

_____ a. Foxes don't swim well.

_____ b. Water is too cold.

_____ c. Ducks catch foxes.

5. Which animal is most like a duck?

_____ a. robin

_____ b. bee

_____ c. fox

6. What will you never see a duck do?

_____ a. climb a big tree

_____ b. eat in the water

_____ c. swim very fast

7. What is the best name for this story?

_____ a. How Ducks Climb

_____ b. How Ducks Catch Bugs

_____ c. Why Ducks Like Water

1. Which is the duck's foot?

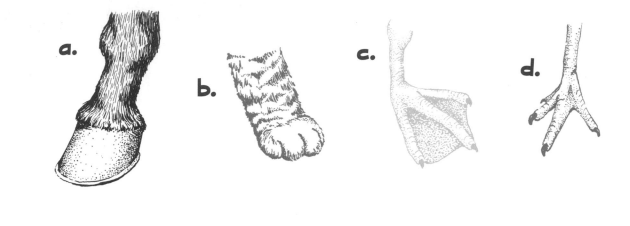

2. Do ducks eat candy?   yes   no

3. Do ducks have four feet?   yes   no

4. Do ducks eat water plants?   yes   no

5. Can ducks read books?   yes   no

6. Do ducks like ponds?   yes   no

7. Do ducks swim on land?   yes   no

8. Do ducks catch bugs?   yes   no

9. Can a fox catch a duck on land?   yes   no

Can you guess the riddles? Circle the right word.

1. I am little.
   I have many feet.
   Ducks eat me.
   Children do not eat me.
   What am I?

   bag bug bird

2. I am an animal.
   I have four feet.
   Ducks must watch
   out for me.
   What am I?

   bug fox bird

Draw lines to match the opposites.
One is done for you.

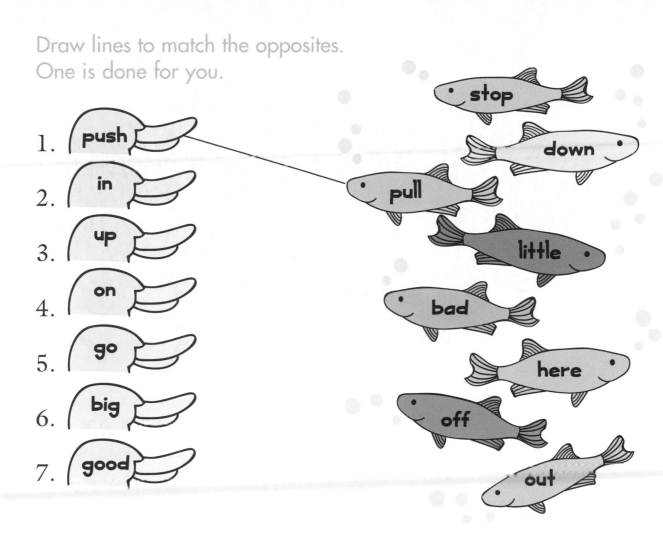

1. push

2. in

3. up

4. on

5. go

6. big

7. good

stop

down

pull

little

bad

here

off

out

Look at a book's Table of Contents page. You can see
the number of the page where each story starts.
Can you answer these?

Stories

1. On which page can you
   find **Fish's Home?** _____

2. What story starts on page 8?
   _____
   _____

3. Is there a story about a turtle
   in this book?
   _____
   _____

A Little Yellow Bird

One night a little yellow bird hopped around. She hopped around in the grass. She looked here and there. She was looking for something to eat. Soon the yellow bird saw a fat worm in the grass. She went to pick up the fat worm.

Just then, a tiger went by. The tiger hid in the tall grass. He looked at the little bird. When the bird pulled at the worm, the tiger jumped! He jumped at the yellow bird! He wanted to eat the bird.

Birds are quick. The little yellow bird got away! She flew far away. The tiger was left with the fat worm.

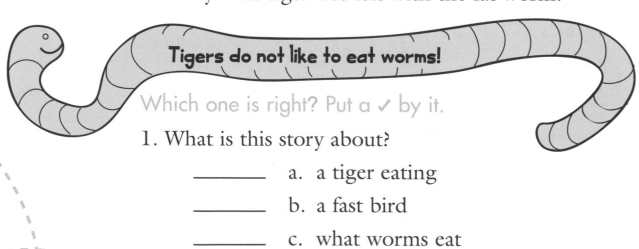

Tigers do not like to eat worms!

Which one is right? Put a ✓ by it.

1. What is this story about?

_____ a. a tiger eating

_____ b. a fast bird

_____ c. what worms eat

2. What was the bird doing?

_____ a. looking for food

_____ b. sitting in a tree

_____ c. looking for a tiger

3. What was the tiger doing?

_____ a. eating worms

_____ b. flying away

_____ c. looking for food

4. Where was the bird?

_____ a. in a tree

_____ b. in a nest

_____ c. in the grass

5. When was the bird looking for food?

_____ a. in the morning

_____ b. in the afternoon

_____ c. at night

6. Who got some food in the story?

_____ a. no one

_____ b. the tiger

_____ c. the bird

7. What color was the bird?

_____ a. brown

_____ b. yellow

_____ c. blue

8. What do you think the worm did?

_____ a. ate the bird

_____ b. got away

_____ c. looked for a tiger

9. A **quick** tiger is a _____ tiger.

_____ a. pretty

_____ b. little

_____ c. fast

10. What is the best name for this story?

_____ a. The Tiger's Dinner

_____ b. How Worms Get Birds

_____ c. The Bird That Got Away

Read the words on the worms. Then read what to do.
Can you mark the right words?

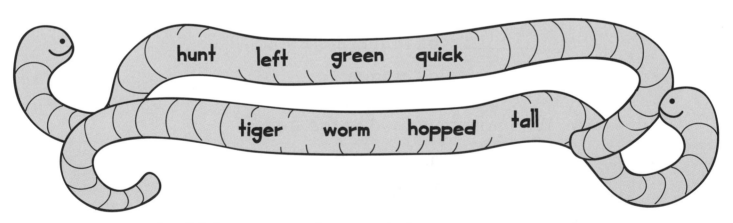

hunt   left   green   quick

tiger   worm   hopped   tall

1. Make a ✔ on the word that means **jumped.**
2. Circle the name of the animal with four feet.
3. Put a box around the color of grass.
4. Put an **X** on the word that means **went away.**
5. Circle the word that means **big.**
6. Put a △ on the word that means **to look for.**
7. Put a line under the word that means **fast.**

Put a ✓ by each one that is right about the story on page 74.

_____ 1. The tiger found some grass to eat.

_____ 2. The worm wanted to eat a fat tiger.

_____ 3. Tigers like to eat worms.

_____ 4. The bird pulled at the worm.

_____ 5. Birds like to eat worms.

_____ 6. The bird got away fast.

_____ 7. The bird picked up the tiger.

_____ 8. The worm was fat.

_____ 9. The tiger hid in the tall grass.

What are Betty Bird and Will Worm doing? Put a ✓
by each sentence that tells what they are doing.

1. _____ a. Betty hunts for food.

_____ b. Betty hops into the water.

_____ c. Betty plays with a tiger.

2. _____ a. Will hid in a box.

_____ b. Will hid in the grass.

_____ c. Will hid in an apple.

3. _____ a. Betty Bird pulls on a worm.

_____ b. Will Worm pulls on a bird.

_____ c. The bird and worm play.

One! Two! Three! Go!

Last Monday, ten children had a race. The race was on the school playground.

Mr. Pack started the race. He told the children to stand side by side.

"Get ready. One! Two! Three! Go!" called Mr. Pack.

Away went the children. They ran faster and faster. Other children saw them run by.

"Hurry! Hurry! Run faster!" the other children called out.

Lupe fell down. Then he could not run again. Pam's shoe came off. She had to stop too! Mr. Pack called, "May wins the race!"

Jeff came in second, with Rita after him. Ted was last in the race.

How did they do in the race? Look at the story again.
Write the names on the lines.

first   second

1. _____   2. _____

next   last

3. _____   4. _____

Which one is right? Put a ✓ by it.

1. What is this story about?

_____ a. Mr. Pack's playground

_____ b. a boat race

_____ c. children in a race

2. When was the race?

_____ a. last Monday

_____ b. last night

_____ c. last Sunday

3. Who watched the race?

_____ a. children

_____ b. fathers

_____ c. mothers

4. Why did Pam stop running?

_____ a. She fell.

_____ b. She saw her friend.

_____ c. Her shoe came off.

5. Who stopped running before the race was over?

_____ a. two girls

_____ b. a boy and a girl

_____ c. two boys

6. How many children ran to the end of the race?

_____ a. ten

_____ b. nine

_____ c. eight

7. Who came in before Rita?

_____ a. Jeff _____ b. Ted _____ c. Bob

8. Who won the race?

_____ a. Rita _____ b. Jeff _____ c. May

9. If you **hurry**, you are _____.

_____ a. sad _____ b. quick _____ c. happy

Draw lines to match these.

1. to go very fast

2. goes on a foot

3. a place to learn

4. after the first

5. looked at

6. made it begin

7. name of a day

8. set to go

9. at the end

10. a place to play

11. a game to see who can go fast

Read each action word. When you put **er** on the action word, you name a person who does the action.

help ⟶ helper   start ⟶ starter
run ⟶ runner   play ⟶ player
win ⟶ winner   jump ⟶ jumper

Circle the right word for each sentence.

1. Mr. Pack will _____ the race.

    start   **starter**

2. May was the _____ of the race.

    win   **winner**

3. There were ten _____ in the race.

    run   **runners**

4. Lupe fell and could not _____ again.

    run   **runner**

Fun time! Can you do this?

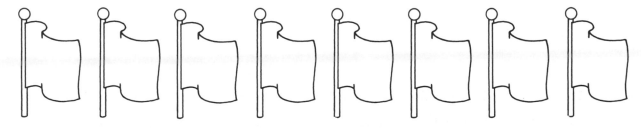

1. How many flags do you see? _____
2. Color the first one blue.
3. Color the last one yellow.
4. Color the second one green.
5. Circle the next to the last one.
6. Color the next to the last one brown.
7. Color four others red.

The Snow Is Too Deep

It snowed all day on Monday. On Tuesday Pat and Bill played in the white snow. They jumped and fell in it.

Bill lost one mitten and some money. Pat lost her ring in the deep, deep snow.

"I want my ring," said Pat. "Please help me find it, Mom!"

Mom said, "No, Pat. The snow is too deep."

"Where is my money?" asked Bill. "No one will help me find it."

Then Dad said, "Soon something big and yellow will help you find the lost things."

On Wednesday, the Sun was in the sky. There was less snow.

On Thursday there was just a little snow. On Friday, the snow was gone. In the mud was a wet mitten! By the fence was a little ring. Bill's money was there too.

What was the children's helper?

Which one is right? Put a ✔ by it.

1. When did the snow start to fall?

_____ a. Monday

_____ b. Wednesday

_____ c. Thursday

2. How do you think Bill's money got lost?

_____ a. Pat hid it in the snow.

_____ b. When Bill fell, the money dropped out.

_____ c. Someone took it out of his mitten.

3. Why didn't Pat find her ring?

_____ a. The trees hid it.

_____ b. Pat left it in her room.

_____ c. The snow was too deep.

4. Where was the ring?

_____ a. under the tree

_____ b. by the fence

_____ c. under the flowers

5. What came first in the story?

_____ a. A mitten was found.

_____ b. Pat asked Mom for help.

_____ c. They played in the snow.

6. What was the children's helper?

_____ a. a truck

_____ b. a moon

_____ c. the Sun

7. What is the best name for this story?

_____ a. Fun in the Mud

_____ b. The Sun and the Snow

_____ c. The Lost Fence

1. not as many

2. something for hands

3. cannot be found

4. falls from the sky

5. the color of snow

6. day after Wednesday

7. a penny

Which one is right? Put a ✓ by it.

1. Three of us came into the room. I came in first. Bill came in last. Pat was _____.

    _____ a. the last one

    _____ b. the first one

    _____ c. the middle one

2. Pat and Bill wanted to go to the zoo on Monday. Mom and Dad had to work on Monday. Dad said they would all go to the zoo the next day. When will they go to the zoo?

    _____ a. on Monday

    _____ b. on Tuesday

    _____ c. on Sunday

Write the days in order.

Friday   Wednesday   Tuesday   Monday   Thursday

1. Sunday   2. _____

3. _____   4. _____

5. _____   6. _____

7. Saturday

Read each story. Circle the words
that tell about the story.

1. The Sun is hot. It helps the trees get big.
   It melts the snow.

   This story is about the _____.

   a. trees   b. Sun   c. flowers

2. On Monday, there was a lot of snow. The Sun came
   out on Tuesday. On Wednesday, there was less snow.
   On Thursday, the snow was gone.

   This story is about _____.

   a. how the snow hid the cars

   b. how deep the snow was

   c. how the snow melted

3. Bill's cat was by the fence. The snow fell. The cat
   ran into the house. Pat had to dry the cat's feet.

   This story is about _____.

   a. wet mittens   b. wet feet   c. wet money

Reading Roundup

All the children are going to a show.
Bev is going to the show on Monday.
Lupe is going the day before Bev.
Jeff is going the day after Bev.
Rita is going the day before Sunday.
Pat is going the day after Tuesday.

When are they going to the show?
Draw lines to match each child to the right day.

1. Pat

2. Rita

3. Bev

4. Lupe

5. Jeff

a. Sunday

b. Monday

c. Tuesday

d. Wednesday

e. Thursday

f. Friday

g. Saturday

Each shelf must have three words.
Put the words below on the right shelves.

Colors
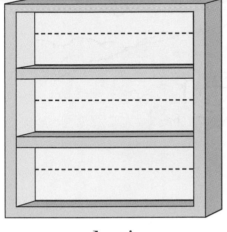

Numbers
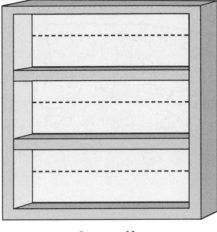

Animals
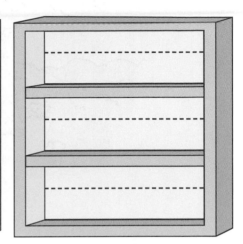

1. tiger
4. worm
7. duck
10. again

2. yellow
5. seven
8. green

3. eight
6. white
9. nine

Draw lines to match these.

1. not as much
2. to look for
3. after the first
4. went away
5. late in the day
6. at the end
7. fast
8. all of them

snow
left
less
evening
hunt
second
every
quick
last

Can you guess the riddles? Circle the right word.

1. I go up, up, up.
   I have grass on me.
   You can run up
   and down on me.
   What am I?

   hill   fox   water

2. I am white.
   I fall from the sky.
   I fall on cold days.
   Children play with me.
   What am I?

   Sun   rain   snow

3. I am wet.
   Fish live in me.
   Children swim in me.
   Ducks sit on me.
   What am I?

   water   hill   box

4. I am a swimmer.
   I like the water.
   I have no feet.
   You like to catch me.
   What am I?

   fox   fish   duck

5. I am little.
   Birds try to get me.
   I have no feet.
   I stay in the grass.
   What am I?

   worm   fox   cat

6. I can run fast.
   I run after birds.
   I have four legs.
   I do not eat worms.
   What am I?

   bug   duck   tiger

Can you do this?

1. Put an **X** on the middle book.

2. Color the top book green.

3. Color the bottom book orange.

4. Make a hole in the bottom.

5. Color the hole brown.

6. Color the shoe yellow.

Circle the one word that fits both sentences.

1. Turn _____ at the corner.

2. The bird _____ in a hurry.

last   left

3. I was _____ in line.

4. The race will _____ a long time.

last   left

Stories

Can you do this?

1. Put an **X** on the page where **Jeff's Ring** starts.

2. Put a line under the story found on page 8.

3. On what page is **A Lost Puppy**? Write it here. _____

The Purple Flower

In the spring, Fay planted seeds in a window box. Pete helped her plant the seeds. They liked the color red. They planted all red flowers.

Little green plants came up first. Then red flowers came out of the green plants. The window box looked very pretty.

Two birds came to the window box. The birds had some seeds in their beaks. One bird dropped a seed. The seed fell into the window box. Fay and Pete did not see the birds.

One day, the children looked at their pretty red flowers. They saw a big purple flower with all the red flowers! What a surprise!

"How did the purple flower get there?" asked Pete.

"I do not know," said Fay. "We planted all red flowers."

They never found out how the purple flower got there. Do you know?

Which one is right? Put a ✔ by it.

1. When did Fay plant seeds in the window box?

   _____ a. fall

   _____ b. winter

   _____ c. spring

2. What is this story about?

   _____ a. a big red flower

   _____ b. what birds eat

   _____ c. a purple surprise

3. What came out of the seeds first?

   _____ a. red flowers

   _____ b. green plants

   _____ c. brown birds

4. Why did the birds have seeds?

   _____ a. to plant them

   _____ b. to eat them

   _____ c. for gifts to the children

5. How did the purple flower get into the box?

   _____ a. Pete planted it there.

   _____ b. Fay put it there as a surprise.

   _____ c. A bird dropped a seed.

6. What is the best name for this story?

   _____ a. A Big Surprise

   _____ b. Pretty Colors

   _____ c. A Nest in the Window Box

Draw lines to match these.

1. time of year

2. made of glass

3. at no time

4. saw where it was

5. a color

6. put seeds in the ground

7. something we did not know about

Circle the right word.

1. Little plants came
| us |
| up |
.

2. Two birds
| can |
| came |
to the window.

3. I saw a seed
| drop |
| chop |
into the box.

4. How did the seed get
| there |
| they |
?

5. They
| every |
| never |
did find out.

Read these sentences.

1. How did the purple flower get here?
2. I did not plant purple flowers.

> The first sentence **asks** something.
> Use a ? at the end.
> The second sentence **tells** something.
> Use a . at the end.

Put ? or . at the end of each sentence.

1. Fay planted some seeds
2. Did Pete help plant seeds
3. Will little green plants come up first
4. Then flowers come out of the plants
5. A seed fell into the window box
6. Did a bird drop the seed

Find the sentence that means the same as the first one. Put a ✔ by it.

1. They planted all red flowers.

   _____ Every flower they planted was red.

   _____ They planted one red flower.

2. Little green plants came up first.

   _____ Little green plants came up after the flowers.

   _____ Little green plants came up before the flowers.

3. The purple flower was a surprise.

   _____ They planted the purple flower.

   _____ They did not know the
   purple flower was there.

The Day Ray Lost Some of His Things

Mr. and Mrs. Hill had three children. Jay was ten years old. Kay was eight. Ray was six years old.

One afternoon, Ray came home from school. He had lost some of his things. He had lost his new book bag! He had lost his lunch box! And he had even lost all the buttons from his coat!

Mrs. Hill said, "Let's help Ray find his things."

The family hunted and looked. Jay found two buttons around the corner. Kay found one button in the doghouse. Mrs. Hill found one button by the flowers. Mr. Hill saw the book bag under a tree. But they did not find the lunchbox.

The next day, Ray went to school again. There was his lunchbox by a window. Ray had left it there.

Which one is right? Put a ✔ by it.

1. How old was Ray?

_____ a. seven

_____ b. four

_____ c. six

2. What is this story about?

_____ a. a lost girl

_____ b. two boys who lost things

_____ c. how the family helped Ray

3. How many buttons were on Ray's coat?

_____ a. four

_____ b. three

_____ c. two

4. Who found the lunchbox?

_____ a. Kay   _____ b. Ray   _____ c. Jay

5. Who found two buttons?

_____ a. Kay   _____ b. Ray   _____ c. Jay

6. Who found the book bag?

_____ a. Mrs. Hill

_____ b. Mr. Hill

_____ c. Kay Hill

7. How did the book bag get under the tree?

_____ a. Kay put it there.

_____ b. Ray put it there and forgot it.

_____ c. The book bag walked there.

8. What must Ray learn to do?

_____ a. stay at home

_____ b. get a new coat

_____ c. take care of his things

Read the story on page 94. Where was each thing found? Draw lines to match them.

THINGS

PLACES

a.

1. around the corner

2. under a tree   b.

3. by the flowers
                        c.

4. in a hole
                        d.

5. in a doghouse

6. at school   e.

Find the sentence that means the same as the first one. Put a ✔ by it.

1. Mr. and Mrs. Hill had three children.

   _____ They had three girls and one boy.

   _____ They had one girl and two boys.

2. Ray left the school at noon.

   _____ He went into the school at noon.

   _____ He came out of the school at noon.

3. They lost the book again.

   _____ They lost the book one more time.

   _____ They never lost the book.

Draw lines to match these.

1. two and one   let's

2. a man   Mr.

3. did not find   button

4. let us   Mrs.

5. noon meal   lost

6. on a coat   three

                                             lunch

Put the words that tell **where** in the **WHERE?** box.
Put the words that tell **when** in the **WHEN?** box.
Draw lines to the right box. The first one is done for you.

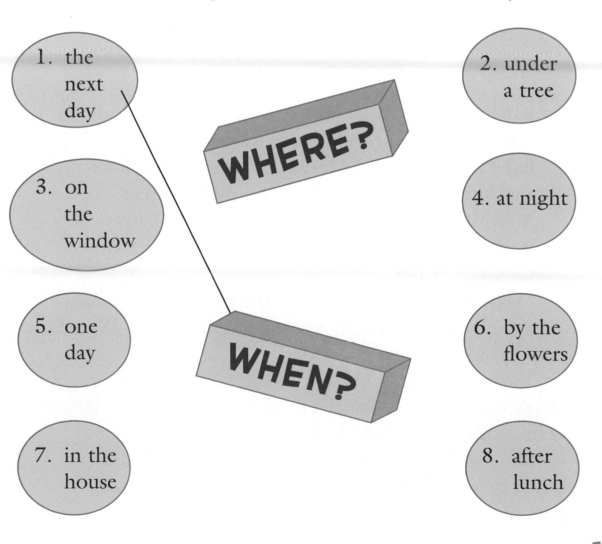

1. the next day

2. under a tree

3. on the window

4. at night

5. one day

6. by the flowers

7. in the house

8. after lunch

WHERE?

WHEN?

Lesson 3

Where Was Baby Seal's Mother?

Baby Seal was asleep on a big rock. Mother Seal was gone. She went to look for food in the water.

Baby Seal got up and looked around. He saw many big mother seals. But he did not see his mother.

A mother seal came up out of the water. Baby Seal barked, "Mother!" He went over to her. The mother seal looked at him.

"You are not my little pup!" she barked. Then Baby Seal began to cry. He looked far out at the sea. Where was his mother?

Two more seals came out of the sea. Baby Seal barked a happy seal bark. He could smell his mother. His mother could smell him.

Baby seals know their mothers. Mother seals know their babies. Now Baby Seal had found his mother.

Which one is right? Put a ✔ by it.

1. This story is about a seal

　　———— a. looking for its home.

　　———— b. looking for its mother.

　　———— c. looking for a hunter.

2. What are baby seals called?

　　———— a. pups

　　———— b. kids

　　———— c. kittens

3. What noise do seals make?

　　———— a. mew　　———— b. bark　　———— c. moo

4. Which one came first?

　　———— a. Baby Seal found his mother.

　　———— b. A seal said, "You are not my pup."

　　———— c. Baby Seal began to cry.

5. Why did Baby Seal cry?

　　———— a. He wanted to go to sleep.

　　———— b. He fell into the cold water.

　　———— c. He wanted to be with his mother.

6. How do mother seals know their babies?

　　———— a. by their smell

　　———— b. by their look

　　———— c. by their cry

Draw lines to match these.

1. baby seal or dog

2. takes care of her children

3. something seals sit on

4. not here

5. a very little child

6. made a dog noise

7. move in the water

8. tell with your nose

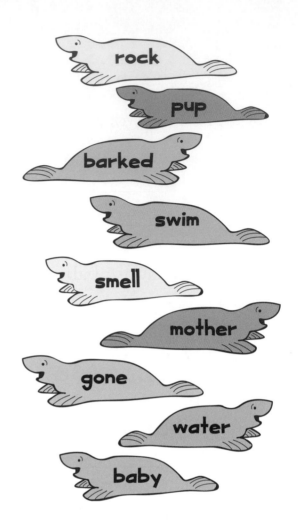

Every sentence has a mark at the end that says "Stop!"
A sentence that **asks** you something has **?** at the end.
A sentence that **tells** you something has **.** at the end.
Put **?** or **.** at the end of each sentence.

1. What did the seals find in the sea

2. Is the water cold

3. The seals barked

4. Is the rock too big to pick up

5. Seals can smell each other

6. Could they see any seals

7. Who began to cry

8. Did they eat many fish

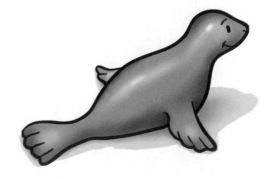

a. Zoo Animals

b. Plants to Grow

c. Work We Do

Look at the three books. Which book would you use to find out about each thing? Write a letter in each box. The first one is done for you.

b	1. flowers that grow fast
	2. how to put out fires
	3. animals that live in water
	4. tigers and monkeys
	5. little trees
	6. cleaning the streets
	7. building a house
	8. seeds of many kinds
	9. working on cars
	10. animals that can fly

Found at the Pond

One afternoon Roy and Rosa were at the pond. Rosa saw something on a water plant. She said, "Here is something funny. What can it be, Roy?"

The thing looked like jelly. It had little black spots in it.

The children put the thing into a big jar with water. They took it home. They watched it every day.

After six days, tadpoles came out of the eggs. They had long tails.

Soon back legs began to come out. The tails got shorter.

Then front legs began to come out. The tails got even shorter.

All four legs got big. The tails were gone!

Rosa said, "Now I know. I found frog eggs. Tadpoles came out of the eggs. Tadpoles are baby frogs!"

Which one is right? Put a ✔ by it.

1. Who found something?

_____ a. a girl   _____ b. a boy   _____ c. a frog

2. Where did they see something funny?

_____ a. in the water

_____ b. in the sand

_____ c. on a shelf

3. What is a tadpole?

_____ a. a baby fish

_____ b. a little duck

_____ c. a little frog

4. What looked like jelly?

_____ a. tadpoles _____ b. frogs _____ c. eggs

5. What came out first?

_____ a. front legs

_____ b. back legs

_____ c. boots

6. What happened to the tadpole?

_____ a. Its tail got very big.

_____ b. It became an egg.

_____ c. It became a frog.

7. What is the best name for this story?

_____ a. What the Frog Found

_____ b. What Rosa Found

_____ c. A Bad Frog

Draw lines to match these.

1. something to hold water

2. the opposite of back

3. used to walk

4. something on the back of animals

5. not as long

6. something to eat on bread

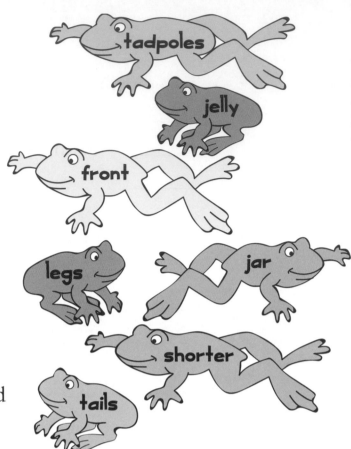

When? Where? Go for a hop with the frog. Put a ✓ on the ones that tell **when**. Put an **X** on the ones that tell **where**.

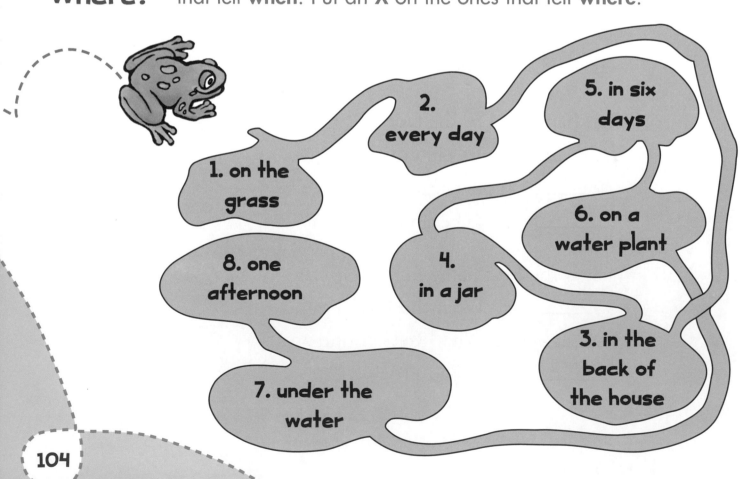

1. on the grass

2. every day

5. in six days

8. one afternoon

4. in a jar

6. on a water plant

7. under the water

3. in the back of the house

Fun time! Read the sentence. Finish it. Circle the right picture.

1. Roy put the funny thing in a _____.

a.

b.

c.

2. They found eggs in the _____.

a.

b.

c.

3. A front door is found on a _____.

a.

b.

c.

4. Roy and Rosa found something that looks like _____.

a.

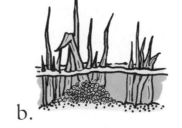
b.

c.

Foxes Looking for Food

One afternoon, a mother fox was out looking for food. Her two little foxes were with her. They saw some ducks in the pond.

Fred Fox said, "I like to eat duck. I wish we could catch one."

Mother Fox said, "We can't catch ducks in the water. They can swim too fast."

The foxes hid in the tall grass. They watched the ducks playing in the pond. At last, eight ducks came out on the land.

Mother Fox said, "Now we can catch a duck. Ducks don't walk fast."

"I'll grab that first duck," said Fran Fox.

"I'll grab that last duck," said Fred Fox.

Mother Fox said, "Wait until they get near us. Ready? Go!" The foxes jumped out of the grass.

As quick as can be, the ducks got away. Did they run away? No! Did they swim away? No! The ducks flew away!

Mother Fox said, "I forgot that ducks have wings. Now we have nothing to eat!"

Which one is right? Put a ✔ by it.

1. Which one happened first?

   _____ a. The foxes jumped at the ducks.

   _____ b. The ducks came out of the water.

   _____ c. The ducks got away.

2. Where did the ducks play?

   _____ a. in the pond

   _____ b. in the barn

   _____ c. in the yard

3. Why did the foxes wait before jumping?

   _____ a. They wanted to surprise the ducks.

   _____ b. They wanted some help.

   _____ c. They wanted Mother Fox to rest.

4. How did the ducks get away?

   _____ a. by walking fast

   _____ b. by jumping in the pond

   _____ c. by flying away

5. What helps a duck fly?

   _____ a. feet

   _____ b. water

   _____ c. wings

6. What is the best name for this story?

   _____ a. A Good Dinner for the Foxes

   _____ b. No Dinner for the Foxes

   _____ c. Fred Fox Gets a Duck

Draw lines to match these.

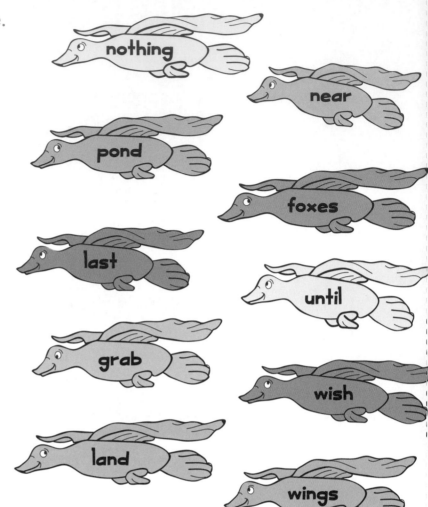

1. not far

2. take away fast

3. not anything

4. water to swim in

5. animals

6. to want

7. up to the time of

8. help birds fly

9. ground

A sentence that tells something ends with . .
A sentence that asks something ends with **?**.
Put **.** or **?** at the end of each sentence.

1. Are you ready to catch a duck

2. The foxes hid in the grass

3. The ducks played in the pond

4. Can foxes catch ducks in the water

5. Did the ducks run away

6. The ducks did not swim away

7. Do ducks have wings

8. Why did the ducks fly away

9. How many ducks did the foxes grab

Find the sentence that means the
same as the first one. Put a ✓ by it.

1. They were by a pond.

_____ a. They were near a fence.

_____ b. They were near the water.

_____ c. They were near the tall grass.

2. Fran walked last.

_____ a. Fran was in the middle.

_____ b. Fran was in back.

_____ c. Fran was first.

Find the sentence that goes with each picture.
Put the right letter under the picture.

1. _____   2. _____   3. _____

a. A duck's feet can push the water.
b. Birds use them to fly.
c. This animal likes to eat ducks.
d. The ducks fly over the pond.

The Best Food

One afternoon Mrs. Giraffe went to the water hole. She went to get a drink. Baby Giraffe did not want to go with her mother.

Mrs. Giraffe said, "Stay here, Baby Pat, and do not go away."

Soon Pat wanted something good to eat. She forgot what her mom told her.

She walked into the tall grass. She saw a fat worm.

Pat wanted to eat the worm. But Pat was too tall. The worm crawled away.

Next Pat saw a little bird on a nest.

"That looks good to eat," said Pat as she bent her long neck to reach the tiny animal.

Surprise! Little birds have wings. The bird flew away. Baby Pat said, "Birds are too fast for me."

She lifted her long neck. Pretty green leaves were right by her mouth. Her mouth opened, and Pat ate the leaves.

Dad Giraffe came by. "Good for you!" he said. "You have found the best food for giraffes. You found it by yourself."

Which one is right? Put a ✔ by it.

1. Which one happened first?

_____ a. The worm crawled away.

_____ b. The giraffe saw a worm.

_____ c. The giraffe ate some leaves.

2. Where did Mom Giraffe go?

_____ a. to the water hole

_____ b. to the big tree

_____ c. to see the bird in the nest

3. Why are leaves the best food for giraffes to eat?

_____ a. The leaves are pretty and are by the water hole.

_____ b. Long necks help giraffes reach leaves on tall trees.

_____ c. Giraffes can reach down to little animals under the grass.

4. What words tell about giraffes?

_____ a. long necks, long legs, wings

_____ b. short back legs, short tail, long fat neck

_____ c. long legs, long neck, spots on fur

5. What is the best name for this story?

_____ a. Dad at the Water Hole

_____ b. A Giraffe Helps Herself

_____ c. Mom Giraffe Finds a Drink

Draw lines to match these.

1. to get up to something

2. very little

3. where to put food

4. to take away fast

5. to move on hands and feet

6. picked up

7. look at something
   for a long time

8. the thing under your head

9. what we do with milk

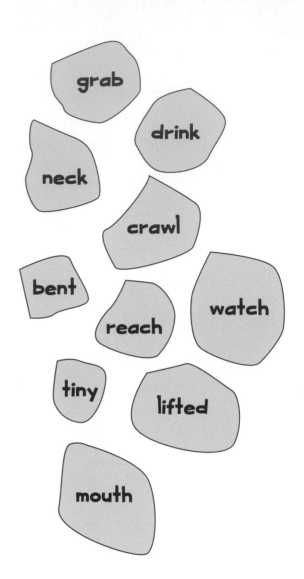

Do the animals eat plants or meat? If they eat other animals, they are meat eaters. Write **plants** next to the plant eaters. Write **meat** next to the meat eaters.

1. _____

2. _____

3. _____

4. _____

Find the sentence that means the same as the first one. Put a ✔ by it.

1. Ray can reach the shelf.

_____ a. He can play with it.

_____ b. He can get to it.

_____ c. He cannot get to it.

2. Baby Giraffe walked in front of the others.

_____ a. She was in the middle.

_____ b. She was the first.

_____ c. She was in back.

3. They lifted a frog.

_____ a. They saw an animal.

_____ b. They picked up an animal.

_____ c. They put down an animal.

Put a ✔ by the words that tell **where**.
Put an **X** by the words that tell **when**.

1. _____ that evening

2. _____ into her pouch

3. _____ before dinner

4. _____ on the leaves

5. _____ on the grass

6. _____ after school

7. _____ all day

8. _____ under the nest

A Bird That Lives on Ice

Look at this animal.
Its feathers look like
a black-and-white suit.
It walks on two feet.
It has a bill.
It cannot fly, but it swims.
Its flippers help it swim.
It is a penguin, a bird
that lives on ice.

It was a dark, cold winter day. Many penguins left the water and met on the ice. The penguins made a lot of noise. They called to each other.

Mr. Penguin called to Mrs. Penguin. Mrs. Penguin heard his voice. They met and walked.

After several days, Mrs. Penguin laid one egg on the ice. It was time to make a nest for the baby penguin egg.

Mr. Penguin rolled the egg onto his two feet. His stomach feathers covered the egg and kept it warm.

Soon Mrs. Penguin called, "Good-bye!" She and the other mother penguins went into the sea. They went to eat fish.

The dads stayed on the ice to care for the eggs. They kept the eggs warm for many weeks. They ate nothing. They got very skinny.

One day, the father penguins were talking.

"Where are the mothers?" one penguin asked. "It's time for the eggs to open."

Another penguin said, "I hope they are safe."

Surprise! The next day, the eggs started to open. The little baby penguins began to make noise. The dads were happy.

But where were the mother penguins?

Which one is right? Put a ✓ by it.

1. Where did Mr. Penguin keep his egg?

_____ a. in the mud

_____ b. on his feet

_____ c. on his bill

2. When did the mother penguins go away?

_____ a. after the babies came

out of the eggs

_____ b. before they laid the eggs

_____ c. after they laid the eggs

3. While the father penguins held their eggs, when did they eat?

_____ a. when it was dark

_____ b. never

_____ c. when they had an egg sitter

4. Where were the mother penguins?

_____ a. getting food from the sea

_____ b. getting skinny

_____ c. at the store getting food

5. What is a good name for this story?

_____ a. A Funny Nest

_____ b. A Nest in a Tree

_____ c. Mother Penguin

Sits on the Eggs

6. When did the penguins meet on the ice?

_____ a. in the winter

_____ b. never

_____ c. when it was warm

7. What is something penguins never do?

_____ a. swim

_____ b. make noises

_____ c. fly

8. What animals eat penguins?

_____ a. horses

_____ b. sharks

_____ c. cows

Draw lines to match these. One is done for you.

1. what your ears did

2. something to put on

3. something very cold

4. very thin

5. what you hear when someone talks

6. what covers all birds

7. more than two

8. where food goes when you eat

ice

stomach

feathers

voice

heard

each

suit

skinny

several

What happened first? Next? Last? Put **1**, **2**, and **3** in the boxes.

☐   Mr. Penguin kept the egg warm.

☐   The egg began to open.

☐   Mrs. Penguin laid an egg.

Circle the right word. One is done for you.

1. The two penguins   men / (met)   there.

2. I heard her   very / voice   .

3. Penguins' feathers look like a   seven / suit   .

4. One egg was laid by   each / reach   bird.

5. The eggs must be   worm / warm   .

6. All birds have feathers and   bills / pills   .

Surprise!

Surprise! The baby penguins came out of the eggs. Another surprise! The same day, the mother penguins came back from the sea. They were fat from eating many fish. They came back to care for the baby penguins.

Mrs. Penguin saw all the dads and baby penguins. They were all making noise. But Mrs. Penguin knew Mr. Penguin's voice. She walked right to him.

Mr. Penguin said, "Meet our new little girl, Penny."

"Oh," said Mrs. Penguin. "What a pretty little baby she is!"

Baby Penny was hungry. Hungry penguin babies peck on their parents' bills. Then the parents put food in the babies' mouths. Mrs. Penguin fed Baby Penny.

"I'm very hungry too," said Mr. Penguin. "Now it's my turn to eat."

"We are too," said all the father penguins. They waved their skinny flippers and said, "Good-bye." They all went into the water to find food.

For two weeks, Mr. Penguin and all the father penguins ate fish. They ate fish night and day. They ate fish heads, fish tails, fish fins, and fish gills. They got round and fat. Their stomachs were full.

Then the fathers were ready to swim home. They were ready to help care for the baby penguins.

A shark saw fat Mr. Penguin swimming home. The shark followed Mr. Penguin.

Mr. Penguin moved down, down into the deep water. The shark went swimming after him.

Quick as a flash, Mr. Penguin zoomed up, up. His flippers moved as fast as the wind.

He rolled onto his stomach. He slid through the water right up to the icy shore.

The hungry shark's mouth opened. He reached for Mr. Penguin's tail feathers. The shark was unlucky. Mr. Penguin, quick as a flash, slid out of the water. He zoomed over the ice on his stomach.

He heard Mrs. Penguin's voice. He heard Baby Penny's voice. He slid right over to them.

Which one is right? Put a ✔ by it.

1. How was Mrs. Penguin different when she came back?

_____ a. She was round and fat.

_____ b. She was very skinny.

_____ c. She was hungry.

2. When did Mr. Penguin go to eat?

_____ a. the week before the egg opened

_____ b. when the egg was on his feet

_____ c. after the egg opened

3. Why did Mr. Penguin go away from Mrs. Penguin?

_____ a. He wanted to play.

_____ b. He needed a new suit.

_____ c. He needed food.

4. Why do you think Mr. Penguin slid on his stomach?

_____ a. His feet hurt.

_____ b. It was quicker than walking on ice.

_____ c. It was the only way he could move.

5. What is the best name for this story?

_____ a. Penny Gets Away from a Shark

_____ b. The Baby Penguin Turns Around

_____ c. Mr. and Mrs. Penguin Take Turns

Write the word to complete the sentence.
Use the words in the box.

flippers	parents	waved
followed	another	

1. The baby _____ his parents.

2. Penguins swim with their _____ .

3. The moms _____ good-bye.

4. Your mom and dad are your _____ .

Read the sentences. Put an **X** next to ones that are
not right. Put a ✓ next to the ones that are right.

_____ 1.   Penguins have warm fur.

_____ 2.   Mother penguins keep the eggs on their feet.

_____ 3.   The parents take turns helping the baby.

_____ 4.   Penguins fly quickly.

_____ 5.   Penguins' feathers are black-and-white.

_____ 6.   The penguin slid on his stomach
                quick as a flash.

Here is a penguin. Draw a line from each word to its picture.

1. bill   2. head

3. stomach   4. flipper

5. feet   6. tail

Circle the right word.

1. The penguins waved their | flippers
                             followed | .

2. Mrs. Penguin did not come back the | some
                                        same | day.

3. Penguins swim quick as a | feather
                              flash | .

4. Fish have | gills
               bills | .

Reading Roundup

Four leaves are on each tree. Put the number of each word on the right tree. The first one is done for you.

ANIMALS   PLACES   NUMBERS

1. sea	2. kangaroo	3. pond
4. giraffe	5. five	6. eight
7. six	8. seal	9. school
10. ten	11. bird	12. doghouse

Draw lines to match these.

1. to pick up

2. to get to it

3. not as long

4. one who works with you

5. up to the time of

6. made a dog noise

7. a baby frog

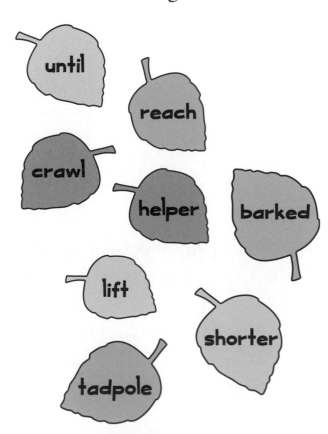

until

reach

crawl

helper   barked

lift

shorter

tadpole

What do you know about foxes and seals?

1. Circle the fox's nose.

2. Put a ✓ on the seal's nose.

Circle **yes** or **no**.

1. Does a kangaroo have two ears?	yes	no
2. Can a tadpole push a car?	yes	no
3. Will a fox eat a bird?	yes	no
4. Do giraffes have wings?	yes	no
5. Do giraffes have long necks?	yes	no
6. Will a seal eat a fish?	yes	no
7. Can a seal fly?	yes	no
8. Do tadpoles have tails?	yes	no
9. Can a seal swim?	yes	no
10. Do seals read fast?	yes	no

Put **?** or **.** at the end of each sentence.

1. How did the purple flower get there

2. What hopped on two big back feet

3. Are the front legs shorter

4. Ray found his lunchbox at school

5. Did the seals eat many fish

6. Baby Seal could smell his mother

7. The giraffe reaches leaves with its long neck

Can you do this?

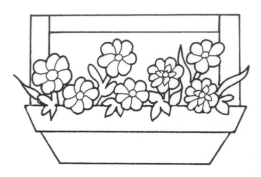

1. Color six flowers purple. Color the other one red.

2. Sara and Dad worked until five o'clock. Show this time on the clock.

3. Here is Ray's coat. Put four green buttons on it.

4. Mother Fox and her little foxes are looking for food. Color the two little foxes brown. Color Mother Fox red.

Put the words that tell **when** in the **WHEN?** box. Put the words that tell **where** in the **WHERE?** box. Draw lines to the right box.

1. at school

2. in the pond

3. long ago

4. in the winter

5. now

6. on the sofa

7. one day

8. next to me

9. after lunch

10. by the sea

Find the sentence that means the same as the first one. Put a ✔ by it.

1. We hunted for the toy.

   _____ a. We played with the toy.

   _____ b. We looked for the toy.

2. Rosa is shorter than Roy.

   _____ a. Rosa is not as tall as Roy.

   _____ b. Rosa is bigger than Roy.

3. The worm crawled to the rock.

   _____ a. The worm reached the rock.

   _____ b. The worm dropped the rock.

Circle the right word.

1. Mother Seal went back to the rock.
   She wanted to _____ for her baby.

   car   care   can

2. Mother frogs lay eggs. Then they go away.
   They _____ see the tadpoles come out.

   ever   every   never

3. Mother came in and found a _____.
   Black spots were on the sofa. Mother saw
   the cat's feet. She knew where the spots came from.

   surprise   nothing   something

Check Yourself

Unit 1

Lesson 1
p. 7
2. yes 5. no
3. yes 6. yes
4. yes 7. yes

p. 8
house: birdhouse,
  cabin, house
food: cherries, ice
  cream, sandwich
people: people making
  cookies, girl in
  rain coat, grandma

Lesson 2
p. 10
1. construction worker
2. jack-in-the-box
3. dad
4. spider
5. mom
6. children and dad
7. mom and dad
8. house

p. 11 (top)
Row 1: Dan, Will
Row 2: Mom, Dad
Row 3: Nan
Row 4: children
Row 5: Jill
(bottom)
1. cannot walk
2. is in a house
3. can eat
4. is new

Lesson 3
p. 13 (top)
2. The Raccoon's Home
(bottom)
1. Food for People
2. The Raccoons Get Food

p. 14
1. no   5. no
2. yes   6. yes
3. yes   7. no
4. yes

Lesson 4
p. 16
1. bee/beehive
2. raccoon/tree
3. bird/nest
4. baby/house
5. bear/cave

p. 17
1. flowers   4. food
2. something 5. good
3. home   6. it
        7. eat

Reading Roundup
p. 18
1. bear
2. bee
3. hills
4. make a new house
5. bugs and flowers

p. 19
Story 1:
2. What Animals Eat
Story 2:
3. Something for Mom
Picture 1:
2. Bees take something
   from flowers.
3. Bees work here.
Picture 2:
1. Dan gets
   something new.
3. Dan sees
   something new here.

Unit 2

Lesson 1
p. 21
1. squirrel
2. bird
3. raccoon
4. children
5. people

p. 22
1. yes   6. yes
2. no   7. no
3. no   8. yes
4. yes   9. no
5. yes   10. yes

Lesson 2
p. 24
2. b
3. b
4. c
5. a

p. 25
1. d
2. c
3. a
4. no picture
5. b

Lesson 3
p. 27
1. Picture b
2. Picture a
3. Picture a
4. Picture b
5. Picture b

p. 28
1. ant
2. bird
3. corn
4. duck
5. bee
6. people
7. ant

Lesson 4
p. 30
2. b   5. a
3. b   6. b
4. a

p. 31
1. bugs
2. fish
3. hill
4. play
5. swim

Reading Roundup
p. 32 (top)
1. duck
2. frog
3. flower
4. fish
5. raccoon
6. grass
(bottom)
3. The Animals
   Have Fun

p. 33 (top)
1. The Fox Will
   Not Eat a Frog
(bottom)
1. fun
2. corn
3. swim
4. you
5. bugs

Unit 3

Lesson 1
p. 35 (top)
c. get food
b. "I will not
   eat a chipmunk."
(bottom)
1. ground
2. run
3. lives

p. 36
1. on the ground
2. happy people
3. two rocks
4. a frog by a flower
5. on the grass
6. is a bird

Lesson 2
p. 38 (top)
2. A Snake in the House
(middle)
1. fast
2. door
3. rocks
(bottom)
Correct Order:
3, 1, 2

p. 39
2. c
3. a
4. a
5. c

Lesson 3
p. 41 (top)
1. c
2. b
(bottom)
1. on a squirrel
2. on a raccoon
3. under a flower
4. on the hill
5. in a spider's home
6. on the corn

p. 42
1. chipmunk
2. fish
3. kids playing
4. ladder

Reading Roundup
p. 43 (top)
2. b
3. a
4. b
(bottom)
1. The Happy People

p. 44 (top)
1. mud
2. a snake
3. away
4. a door
5. bugs
6. a hill
(bottom)
1. a
2. b

p. 45 (top)
1. happy
2. fast
3. want
(bottom)
Correct Order:
3, 2, 1

Unit 4

Lesson 1
p. 47
2. a
3. b
4. c
5. b
6. c

p. 48 (top)
2. new
3. hop
4. back
5. finger
6. paws

p. 48 (bottom)
2. paw
3. back
4. pouch
5. tail
6. front

p. 49
2. It
3. She
4. It
5. He
6. They
7. It

Lesson 2
p. 51
2. b
3. a
4. c
5. c

p. 52 (top)
1. new
2. food
3. swim
4. pond
5. fun
6. walk
(bottom)
1. Ducks swim.
2. The duck walks
   with Mother
   Duck.
3. A duck is eating.

p. 53 (top)
2. It
3. They
4. She
5. He
(bottom)
Correct order:
2, 3, 1

Lesson 3
p. 54
1. c
2. b

p. 55
3. c   6. c
4. a   7. b
5. b   8. b

p. 56 (top)
2. morning
3. robin
4. Mrs.
5. oak
6. blue
7. Mr.
8. nest

126

(bottom)
1. The oak tree is big.
2. Three eggs are in the nest.
3. The robin finds some grass.

p. 57 (top)
1. them
2. They
3. him
4. it
5. Her
(bottom)
Correct order:
3, 2, 1

Lesson 4
p. 58
1. a

p. 59
2. c   5. b
3. a   6. a
4. c   7. c

p. 60 (top)
2. forgot
3. lettuce
4. milk
5. money
6. children
7. afternoon
8. corner
(bottom)
2. house
3. walk
4. girl
5. black

p. 61 (top)
1. It
2. them
3. They
4. He
5. him
(bottom)
Correct order:
2, 1 3

Reading Roundup
p. 62 (top)
1. four
2. zero
3. zero
4. four
5. four
6. zero
7. zero
8. four
(bottom)
1. He
2. They
3. them

p. 63 (top)
1. pouch
2. food
3. afternoon
4. again
5. park
6. night
7. front
(bottom)
1. c
2. b
3. b

p. 64 (top)
1. hop
2. grass, mud
3. tub
4. forgot
5. back
6. money
7. grass
(bottom)
Correct order:
2, 3, 1

p. 65
1. d
2. c
3. b
4. e
5. a

Unit 5

Lesson 1
p. 66
1. c

p. 67
2. b   5. b
3. a   6. a
4. b   7. b

p. 68 (top)
1. seven
2. bottom
3. Sunday
4. evening
5. eight
6. shelf
7. every
8. toys
9. middle
(bottom)
Color and place objects
on shelves as directed.

p. 69 (top)
1. top
2. top
3. play
4. play
5. care
6. care

(bottom)
1. Bill
2. Bev
3. Bob
4. Bob
5. Bev
6. Bev

Lesson 2
p. 70
1. c

p. 71
2. c   5. a
3. b   6. a
4. a   7. c

p. 72 (top)
1. c
2. no
3. no
4. yes
5. no
6. yes
7. no
8. yes
9. yes
(bottom)
1. bug
2. fox

p. 73 (top)
2. out
3. down
4. off
5. stop
6. little
7. bad
(bottom)
1. 4
2. Rabbit's House
3. no

Lesson 3
p. 74
1. b

p. 75
2. a   5. c
3. c   6. a
4. c   7. b

p. 76 (top)
8. b
9. c
10. c
(bottom)
1. hopped
2. tiger
3. green
4. left
5. tall
6. hunt
7. quick

p. 77 (top)
4, 5, 6, 8, 9
(bottom)
1. a
2. c
3. a

Lesson 4
p. 78
1. May
2. Jeff
3. Rita
4. Ted

p. 79
1. c   4. c
2. a   5. b
3. a   6. c

p. 80 (top)
7. a
8. c
9. b
(bottom)
1. hurry
2. shoe
3. school
4. second
5. watched
6. started
7. Monday
8. ready
9. last
10. playground
11. race

p. 81 (top)
1. start
2. winner
3. runners
4. run
(bottom)
1. 8
Color the flags in this order:
blue, green, red, red, red,
red, brown, yellow.
Circle the brown flag.

Lesson 5
p. 82
1. a

p. 83
2. b   5. c
3. c   6. c
4. b   7. b

p. 84 (top)
1. less
2. mittens
3. lost
4. snow
5. white
6. Thursday
7. money
(bottom)
1. c
2. b

p. 85 (top)
2. Monday
3. Tuesday
4. Wednesday
5. Thursday
6. Friday
(bottom)
1. b
2. c
3. b

Reading Roundup
p. 86
1. d
2. g
3. b
4. a
5. c

p. 87 (top)
Colors:
yellow, white, green
Numbers:
eight, seven, nine
Animals:
tiger, worm, duck
(bottom)
1. less
2. hunt
3. second
4. left
5. evening
6. last
7. quick
8. every

p. 88
1. hill
2. snow
3. water
4. fish
5. worm
6. tiger

p. 89 (top)
Put an X on the middle
book, color the top
book green, color the
bottom book orange,
make a brown hole in
the bottom of the shoe,
and color the shoe yel-
low.
(middle)
1. left
2. left
3. last
4. last
(bottom)
1. Put an x on 3.
2. Underline
The Ice Melts
3. 6

Unit 6

Lesson 1

p. 91
1. c   4. b
2. c   5. c
3. b   6. a

p. 92 (top)
1. spring
2. window
3. never
4. found
5. purple
6. plant
7. surprise
(bottom)
1. up
2. came
3. drop
4. there
5. never

p. 93 (top)
1. .   4. .
2. ?   5. .
3. ?   6. ?
(bottom)
1. Every flower they planted was red.
2. Little green plants came up before the flowers.
3. They did not know the purple flower was there.

Lesson 2

p. 94
1. c

p. 95
2. c   6. b
3. a   7. b
4. b   8. c
5. c

p. 96 (top)
1. c
2. d
3. a or e
4. no match
5. a or e
6. b
(bottom)
1. They had one girl and two boys.
2. He came out of the school at noon.
3. They lost the book one more time.

p. 97 (top)
1. three
2. Mr.
3. lost
4. let's
5. lunch
6. button

(bottom)
Where: 2, 3, 6, 7
When: 1, 4, 5, 8

Lesson 3

p. 99
1. b   4. b
2. a   5. c
3. b   6. a

p. 100 (top)
1. pup
2. mother
3. rock
4. gone
5. baby
6. barked
7. swim
8. smell
(bottom)
1. ?   5. .
2. ?   6. ?
3. .   7. ?
4. ?   8. ?

p. 101
2. c   7. c
3. a   8. b
4. a   9. c
5. b   10. a
6. c

Lesson 4

p. 102
1. a

p. 103
2. a   5. b
3. c   6. c
4. c   7. b

p. 104 (top)
1. jar
2. front
3. legs
4. tails
5. shorter
6. jelly
(bottom)
Put a ✓ on 2, 5, 8.
Mark X on 1, 3, 4, 6, 7.

p. 105
1. b
2. c
3. b
4. b

Lesson 5

p. 107
1. b   4. c
2. a   5. c
3. a   6. b

p. 108 (top)
1. near
2. grab
3. nothing
4. pond
5. foxes
6. wish
7. until
8. wings
9. land
(bottom)
1. ?   6. .
2. .   7. ?
3. .   8. ?
4. ?   9. ?
5. ?

p. 109 (top)
1. b
2. b
(bottom)
1. c
2. b
3. a

Lesson 6

p. 111
1. b
2. a
3. b
4. c
5. b

p. 112 (top)
1. reach
2. tiny
3. mouth
4. grab
5. crawl
6. lifted
7. watch
8. neck
9. drink
(bottom)
1. meat
2. meat
3. plants
4. plants

p. 113 (top)
1. b
2. b
3. b
(bottom)
Put a ✓ by 2, 4, 5, 8.
Mark X by 1, 3, 6, 7.

Lesson 7

p. 115
1. b
2. c
3. b
4. a
5. a

p. 116 (top)
6. a
7. c
8. b
(bottom)
2. suit
3. ice
4. skinny
5. voice
6. feathers
7. several
8. stomach

p. 117 (top)
Correct order: 2, 3, 1
(bottom)
2. voice
3. suit
4. each
5. warm
6. bills

Lesson 8

p. 119
1. a
2. c

p. 120 (top)
3. c
4. b
5. c
(bottom)
1. followed
2. flippers
3. waved
4. parents

p. 121 (top)
1. X
2. X
3. ✓
4. X
5. ✓
6. ✓
(middle)
Make sure the lines were drawn to the correct parts of the penguin.
(bottom)
1. flippers
2. same
3. flash
4. gills

Reading Roundup

p. 122 (top)
Animals: 2, 4, 8, 11
Places: 1, 3, 9, 12
Numbers: 5, 6, 7, 10
(bottom)
1. lift
2. reach
3. shorter
4. helper
5. until
6. barked
7. tadpole

p. 123 (top)
Circle the fox's nose.
Check the seal's nose.

(middle)
1. yes
2. no
3. yes
4. no
5. yes
6. yes
7. no
8. yes
9. yes
10. no

(bottom)
1. ?
2. ?
3. ?
4. .
5. ?
6. .
7. .

p. 124
1. Color six flowers purple and one flower red.
2. Draw hands to 5 o'clock.
3. Add four green buttons to the coat.
4. Color the little foxes brown and the Mother Fox red.
(bottom)
When: 3, 4, 5, 7, 9
Where: 1, 2, 6, 8, 10

p. 125 (top)
1. b
2. a
3. a
(bottom)
1. care
2. never
3. surprise